Traditional
Chinese Clothing

Costumes, Adornments & Culture

Shaorong Yang

LONG RIVER PRESS
San Francisco

2009002547

Editorial Committee
Art Adviser: Yang Xin, Wang Qingzheng & Zhang Daoyi
Chief Editor: Wu Shiyu
Deputy Chief Editor: Ma Ronghua & Dai Dingjiu
Editorial Committe Members: Qian Gonglin, Lin Lanying, Zhang Debao &
Wushaohua
Author: Yang Shaorong
Executive Editor: Dai Dingjiu
Designer: Lu Quangen
Photographer: Ding Guoxing
Introduction: Tang Weikang
Translators: Ding Shaohong & Li Shanshan
English Editor: Luo Tianyou

First Edition 2004

ISBN 1-59265-019-8

Library of Congress Cataloging-in-Publication Data

Yang, Shaorong.
[Fu shi. English]
Chinese clothing : costumes, adornments, culture / [by Yang Shaorong]
        p. cm. — (Arts of China ; #1)
ISBN 1-59265-019-8
1. Costume—China—History. 2. Clothing and dress—China—History.
3. China—Social life and customs. I. Title. II. Series: Arts of China
GT1555.Y3313 2003
391'.00951—dc22

2003016727

Published in the United States of America by
Long River Press
3450 3rd St., #4B, San Francisco, CA 94124
www.longriverpress.com
in association with Shanghai People's Fine Arts Publishing House

Printed in China

10 9 8 7 6 5 4 3 2 1

Table of Contents

Introduction

With the development of China's economy and culture, the requirements for dress and its varied adornments have evolved over a period of several thousand years. It was from the Xia and Shang dynasties that a systematic structure of clothing use came into being in China, where factors such as color, design, and rules governing use were implemented across social classes from the emperor to the common people.

China is a multi-ethnic country. Each ethnic minority of China retains its indigenous culture. The mutual support and inspiration among these nationalities have contributed to the rich textures and fabrics of history and have made Chinese dress as a whole all the more varied and glorious.

During the Sui and Tang Dynasties, China's economy prospered, reaching a "Golden Age" of philosophical and artistic development, cultural enlightenment, and prosperity. The people of China's central plains gathered in Changan and Luoyang to promote cultural exchange, and the fabrics and dress of central Asia greatly influenced the development of the majority, or "Han" Chinese dress.

A rigid set of rules and guidelines for dress was characteristic of China's dynastic period: yellow was the most prosperous color and could only be worn by the emperor. Green, red, white, and black symbolized the East, South, West, and North respectively. Green, red, black, white, and yellow are pure colors which were assigned to and by the emperor and gentry class. The geometric patterns, animals, and floral patterns were widely adopted in dress and adornments and have evolved over a period of several thousand years. Symmetry of design, balance, layout, and composition are defining characteristics of Chinese clothing.

This book serves as an introduction to some of the many varieties of traditional Chinese clothing, dress, and costume adornments. The articles of clothing of past dynasties are but one chapter of China's long history. They reflect the economic and political life of past centuries, and provide valuable insight into ancient life in everyday China.

1. The Culture of Chinese Clothing

The story of clothing and costumes is one of the most fascinating developments in human history.

Clothing is the result of a unique kind of endeavor undertaken by humans. It is a "material" product, but it is also significant in terms of the cultural progression of humanity. Human society has marched for hundreds and thousands of years from the prehistoric age to the twenty-first century. After being exposed to the elements, human ancestors understood the function and utility of protective garments, and adapted them to fit specific situations.

The pursuit of beauty is also in the nature and development of human society: the function of clothing lies not only in protection but also in beauty. Since the origin of clothing and protective garments, people have been combining and integrating clothes into the development of customs, colors, culture, and religion.

Clothing in China has been shaped and has developed alongside the interactive influences between the outside world and China's own dynastic traditions. Since the Han (206 B.C.-A.D. 220) and Tang (618-907) dynasties, Chinese clothing has absorbed and merged favorable elements in foreign cultures before developing into an integrated system of textile manufacturing culture with the Han nationality as the primary component. In order to understand the varied styles, unique charm, bright colors, and exquisite techniques, one should first know about the history of the development of Chinese clothing, and by doing so explore the subtleties of Chinese history and culture.

In the Shang Dynasty (1600-1046 B.C.), with the development of social productivity, there were clearly visible signs of material culture. In the inscriptions on bones or tortoise shells—called "oracle bones" there were pictographs for mulberry, cocoons, and silk, which showed the development of one of the earliest forms of Chinese agriculture. Silk prints with patterns and silk fabric pieces decorating bronze weapons showed the advancement and elegance of techniques used in textiles alongside those used in wood and bronze pieces usually associated with that historical period. The pictographs also feature differentiation of clothing for various social classes such as rulers, gentry, slaves, etc.

During the Zhou Dynasty (1046-256 B.C.), the Chinese clothing system was gradually improved. At that time, many inscriptions and patterns were made on clothing. With hierarchy and social status came a set of systems for clothing reflected in religious or sacrificial duties, court robes, military clothing, marriage, and ancestor worship.

During the Warring States Period (475-221 B.C.), many regions chose not to follow the system of the Zhou Dynasty. Seven regions became independent. As the Qin Kingdom was in the west of China, for example, it utilized a different system of clothing when compared to its neighbors. Part of the reason for this was to differentiate various armies loyal to a particular commander. It was the time of the "Hundred Schools of Thought" in Chinese history. Commanders and military strategists espoused their individual philosophies: Lord Chunshen's retinue all wore pearled shoes; Lord Pingyuan's concubines and their maids wore damask; soldiers guarding King Wei's palace wore black military suits; while scholars wore fine thin silk, long robes and square shoes.

According to the Spring and Autumn Annals and other historical records of the Warring States Period, "the minor nationalities made clothes" during the reign of the Yellow Emperor. This was normally a prosperous period for matriarchal clans. Spinning wheels, bone needles, rope pendants and textile pieces of that time have since been unearthed and are the subject of great study and admiration. Pottery paintings unearthed in Gansu Province show the functionality of jackets and skirts worn by both men and women in ancient China.

The clothing system at the beginning of the Han Dynasty offered no restrictions on clothing worn by the common people. In the Western Han Dynasty (206 B.C.-A.D. 25), although the emperors gave decrees on general clothing use, their edicts were not specific enough to be restrictive to the populace, nor were they enforced to any great degree. For the most part, clothing simply differed according to season, for example: blue colors for spring, red for summer, yellow for autumn and black for winter. Women of the Han Dynasty commonly wore jackets and skirts in a variety of colors throughout the year.

Since the time of the Kingdom of Wei (220-265), the Jin Dynasty (25-420) and the Southern and Northern Dynasties (420-589), many of those in China's northern hinterland came to live in China's heartland, bringing their styles of clothing with them. At the same time, their indigenous clothing also influenced and was assimilated into Han culture.

After the Sui Dynasty (581-618), the familiar clothing system characteristic of China's Han nationality was established in earnest. However, the influence imposed by the aforementioned northern minorities remained highly influential. It was not until the Tang Dynasty that a system of clothing maintaining the continuity of the Han system was established, due in large part to the prosperity and stability of the Tang, where great social and cultural exchanges were undertaken between the capital and China's northern borders.

During the Tang it was commonplace for people of that time to wear clothes and fineries of China's many ethnic minorities. In the Sui and Tang dynasties women usually wore jackets, coats, blouses, and skirts. Red skirts were the most popular and auspicious color, as well as purple, yellow, and green. The front portion of a woman's shoe was generally in the shape of a phoenix. Many women, including maids and courtesans, also wore boots with red silk. Daily clothing encompassed a wide variety of uses: coats, jackets, robes, waist cloth, skirts, trousers, short trousers, socks, shoes, and boots.

In the Song Dynasty (960-1279), a sizeable amount of territory in the north was seized by the Nuchen people, and thus the culture of clothing now interacted due to political, economic, and geographic factors. In the work *Sequel to History as a Mirror*, it is stated: "In the Lin'an Prefecture, since the last decade, there had been an abnormal clothing system and people were used to wearing clothes of minor nationalities." Even in the capital city of the Southern Song Dynasty (1127-1279), northern-style clothing was still quite popular. Familiar fabric included gauze, brocade, damask, and crepe. Skirts in particular were unique with gauze as the most common fabric, and pomegranate red as the most popular color. Pleated skirts were also introduced and were characteristic of higher social classes.

The Yuan Dynasty (1206-1368) was a period of time when Mongols conquered and ruled the Chinese empire. In addition to offering its own characteristic style of clothing, the Yuan Dynasty carried on with the clothing and costumed traditions of the Han Dynasty. At first, scholars and civilians at the Mongol capital were ordered to wear Mongol-type clothes, including hats made of bamboo, beginning around 1297, scholars of Mongolian and Han nationality were free to wear the style of clothes that pleased them. As for women's clothing, fur and leather, commonplace among Mongol clothes, were introduced to China on a wide scale. In general, suede and felt were the materials common in clothes and hats. Gowns were loose and long and often used for ceremonial occasions. By the close of the Yuan Dynasty, the clothing of Korea was seen as especially beautiful, and clothes, boots, and hats similar to the style of Korea were popular and adopted among the Mongol rulers.

After Zhu Yuanzhang established the Ming Dynasty (1368-1644), any non-Han clothing, language and surnames, were banned. Later an imperial decree was issued which stated that the clothing system would follow that established during the Tang Dynasty. During the Ming, the style and protocol for the emperor, court officials, royal servants, and other members of the imperial household, was incredibly detailed and elaborate.

For everyday clothing, an even more intricate series of regulations were stipulated. An imperial decree was given to declare that "Those who are dressed in a non-Han way shall be seriously punished." During the Chongzhen Period (1628-1644), the Emperor ordered the crown prince and other imperial family members to wear blue cloth coats, purple printed cloth waistcoats, white cloth trousers, indigo cloth skirts, white cloth socks, blue cloth shoes and black coifs. This change reflected civilians' clothing at the time. In daily life, women were limited to wearing plain, unadorned fabrics of purple or peach hues without any gold embroidery. Robes were often of soft, light colors instead of pure reds, blacks or yellows. Broad belts were made of indigo silk cloth. Buttons appeared with great frequency during the Ming era, while women's shoes were still in the shape of a phoenix's head with pearls, and sometimes with a cloud design embroidered with little golden flowers.

Like the Yuan Dynasty, the Qing (or Manchu) Dynasty (1644-1911), marked the return of a non-Han minority to the seat of power in China. Like the Mongols of the Yuan Dynasty, the people were forced to alter their hair and change their clothes according to the Manchu custom. One of the most visible signs of this was the combing back and braiding of men's hair into the queue, or pigtail.

The characteristics of Ming-era clothing were maintained for a long period of time. Although during the Qing Dynasty attempts were repeatedly made to abolish outright the clothing system of the Ming Dynasty, official badges of rank and ceremonial clothes adopted their design.

The clothing of the gentry class in the Qing Dynasty were displayed in hat buttons, feathers, and badges which contained an embroidered pattern of a particular animal. First in importance came the emperor; the imperial family, officials with ranks from Level 1 (highest) to Level 9 (lowest), and civil servants who had passed the imperial examinations at various levels. There were also Rank 1, 2 and 3 for members of the imperial retinue, with blue feathers as decoration, the emperor's near official as servants, etc. In all cases, the rank and clothing of these individuals was strictly dictated.

Men's clothing in the Qing Dynasty consisted for the most part of long silk gowns and the so-called "Mandarin" jacket, which perhaps achieved their greatest popularity during the latter Kangxi Period (1662-1722) to the Yongzheng Period (1723-1736).

For women's clothing, Manchu and Han systems of clothing coexisted. Manchu women mostly wore long gowns while Han women still considered coats and skirts fashionable. Since the middle of the Qing, the Manchu and Han nationalities were integrated but maintained the unique characteristics of their respective clothing styles. In the latter Qing, a fashion trend emerged whereby Manchu people began to imitate clothing of the Han. However, the fashion of Han people imitating Manchu clothing also prevailed at that time among the gentry and aristocratic classes.

Beginning in the middle 1840s, China entered the modern era. After the Opium War, foreign nations established the treaty port system along China's coastline, and numerous westerners began to live and work in ever increasing numbers. Western culture began to permeate Chinese culture.

In Shanghai, which became at that time the center of commerce in China, Westerners and Chinese lived and worked in close proximity, and there clothing experienced its first revolution. Initially, there was little variety in terms of clothing styles. Chinese men still wore the characteristic long gowns and mandarin jackets, while women still wore skirts or gowns. With the increasing prosperity of commerce and trade, foreign products began to pour in, such as camlet (a combination of silk and camel's hair), woolen cloth, foreign silk, and printed cloth, bringing with it a shift in traditional Chinese clothing. The foreign clothes gradually won popularity among urban dwellers. The labor-intensive method of traditional Chinese clothing gave way to western needlework, and, ultimately, machine-manufacturing began to prevail.

In women's fashion in particular, the advent of mechanized textile manufacturing had significant influence in the elegantly-sewed and fashionable styles of the early twentieth century. The *qipao* (or *cheongsam*) popular in the 1920s, originated from traditional Manchu women's clothing, and its design and style were altered by Han women after continual improvement and evolution with western clothing styles.

The *qipao* was immensely popular for more than twenty years, from the 1920s to the close of the 1940s, and was subject to several shifts in style, such as the height of collar, cut of sleeve and height of vent at the sides, the latter of which changed forever the image of Chinese women. The *qipao* addressed fashion concerns at that time and was certainly viewed as an iconic garment in the increasing level of freedom experienced by urban-dwelling Chinese women. Blue cloth *qipaos* were most popular among female students, and its popularity quickly spread across the country, becoming the typical clothing of new Chinese women in the late 1920s. Cosmopolitan women and film stars in Shanghai promoted development of the *qipao* by making many innovations in its style. From the 1930s, the *qipao* was considered standard clothing for Chinese women. Civilian women, female students and workers, as well as senior officials' wives all wore *qipaos*, which became standard for social events and diplomatic functions. Later, the *qipao* spread to foreign countries and became a fashion icon. Today it can still be seen at weddings and other festive occasions.

2. Hats and Headdresses

Coronet — Hats worn by ancient kings or senior officials for ceremonial events and in matters of protocol. It is said that coronets originated from the Yellow Emperor. Coronets fall into six categories, and are matched with accompanying clothing as dictated by a particular occasion. After the Song Dynasty, officials no longer wore coronets. Coronets were last used during the Ming Dynasty. After more than two thousand years of use, coronets were at last abolished during the Qing Dynasty.

Phoenix hat — Ceremonial headdresses worn by women. Phoenix hats in the Ming Dynasty had two forms: the first was worn by empresses and imperial concubines and were decorated with the designs of dragons, golden pheasants, and, of course, the phoenix. The other types were colored hats worn by women of official rank; these were decorated with pearls, golden pheasants, and flower-shaped hair pins. In the Ming and Qing dynasties the colored hats worn by civilian women during the wedding ceremony were also referred to as phoenix hats.

Gugu hat — A type of hat worn by Mongolian noblewomen during the Yuan Dynasty. Gugu was the Mongolian word for hat, which was translated into Chinese according to its pronunciation. At that time, Gugu hats could only be worn by Mongolian noblewomen. Gugu hats were made of iron wires and bamboo strips, and took the shape of a large flask.

Court hat — A hat matching the imperial robes, worn during ceremonial occasions. During the Qing Dynasty, only emperors, expresses, princes, dukes, officials, and women with rank given by the emperor were allowed to wear the court hat. There were court hats for winter and for summer. The winter hats were made of fur and had a hunch top, red tassels, and pearls. The summer hats were made of vines and bamboo thread. On the sides of the hat there was a string to be tied under the chin. The court hats worn by officials were differentiated by their appearance to denote rank within the imperial

A coronet-shaped hat (Qing Dynasty)

Children's hat
(Zhejiang Province)

A hat of the Yi
nationality (Yunnan
Province)

retinue. According to imperial regulations, gems and precious metals were placed at the top of court hats in the form of a "button" to indicate their respective rank from lowest to highest, for example: rubies for Rank 1; coral for Rank 2; sapphire for Rank 3; lapis lazuli for Rank 4; crystal for Rank 5; tridacna shell for Rank 6; gold for Rank 7; intaglio carved gold for Rank 8; and relief carved gold for Rank 9. During the later years of the Qing Dynasty, colored glass was used instead of actual gemstones, and the buttons were thus called respectively Bright Red Top for Rank 1; Dark Red Top for Rank 2; Bright Blue Top for Rank 3; Dark Blue Top for Rank 4; Bright White Top for Rank 5; Dark White Top for Rank 6. Gold Top was later replaced by bronze for Rank 7.

Wire hat — A hat where the front is lower with a seam in front, iron wires inside, and silk ribbon decoration outside the seam. The wired hat originated in the Han Dynasty. The number of wires and the ribbons corresponded with rank. There were seven wires, a jade belt, and four-colored ribbon with the design of clouds and phoenix for Rank 1; six wires, a rhinoceros horn belt, and a Rank 1 ribbon for Rank 2; five wires, gold belt and ribbon with the design of clouds and crane for Rank 3; four wires, Rank 3 belt, and ribbon for Rank 4; three wires, silver belt, and ribbon with round patterns for Rank 5; two wires, silver belt and three-colored ribbon with the design of magpies for Rank 6 and 7; and one wire, horn belt, and ribbon with the design of pheasants for Rank 8 and 9. The number of wires was added on the basis of the Tang and Song system.

Black gauze hat—A round official's hat made of black gauze originating in the Sui Dynasty. Black gauze hats in the Song Dynasty evolved from the Tang Dynasty. The soft wings were now hardened. In the Ming Dynasty, officials who were present at the imperial court were required to wear these hats, together with robes and various badges as decoration. Number One Scholars and successful candidates in the highest level of the imperial examinations could also wear such hats. At first the black gauze hat was made with wool inside, which was wrapped with gauze and colored with black paint. The lining was made of vine fibers or hemp. Two straight wings with round corners were added to either side, tied with iron wires. There were two ribbons at the back of the hat and a mesh inside to wrap the hair. The two wings stretched out on both sides and the length totaled approximately one foot, although some were wider.

Curtain hat — A type of hat with high top and broad hem also called a mat hat. There is a mesh veil around the hem which extends back to the neck. This was first worn by people in China's western regions. The curtain hat was often used as a shield against the elements.

Little hat—A daily hat worn by officials in the Qing Dynasty. Because the hat is made with six separate pieces it is also called the "6-in-1 hat." Gauze is used in summer and autumn and damask is used in spring and winter. The color is mostly black. The inside is red. There is a knot at the top made by red threads. For common people, the knot is black. On occasions of funerals, the knot is white. The Little hat was a popular and everyday sight from the time of the late Ming Dynasty to the end of the Republican era (1949).

Summer hat — Ceremonial hat worn by men during the Qing Dynasty. The summer hat was regulated in the official clothing system as a hat to be worn during the summer. It is in the shape of a circular cone, sometimes resembling a trumpet. There is a pearl or red tassel on top. The inside was made by using dried animal bladder, vines, bamboo, or wheat straw. The outside is covered with damask, usually in white, blue, and yellow. The lining is red silk and the side is white. There is a ring inside the hat to fit the head. Two fabric strips are beside the ring for tying. There is a plume tube made of white jade, emerald, or glass under the top pearl so as to fit a blue or colored plume: a blue plume is made of pheasant feather and does not have any "eyes," while a colored plume is made of peacock feather and has one, two, or three eyes, which refers to the round colored pattern at the end of peacock feathers, indicating nobility. The summer hat originated from traditional Manchu customs, which were usually made using grass.

Head banner —Worn by women in the late Qing Dynasty. Originally intended for Manchu noblewomen and civilian women, often worn at wedding ceremonies. Affected by a Han hairstyle, the head banner gradually came into shape. After the Xianfeng Period (1851-1861), it developed into a fixed tall decoration, which could be simply put on the head with some silk flowers. It was not until the seventh or eighth year of the Republican era that the head banner ceased being worn.

Children' s hat — Children' s hats were made of cotton. They can be lovely, elegant, and meaningful. These hats often denote luck and peace if worn by children on holidays or birthdays. The hats could be in the shape of a tiger, carp, rabbit, dragon, or phoenix. Silver decorations with the design featuring the Eight Immortals were usually applied to the front for good luck. Many of these hats are still worn today.

Children' s hat (Sichuan Province)

Arhat hat (Hunan
Province)

A hat worn by
scholar

3. Clothes

Coronet suit — A suit worn by emperors, kings and lords on ceremonial occasions. A coronet hat matched the coronet suit. The coronet suit included a black coat and a light red skirt and was decoration with the style of the Twelve Seals. The coronet suit originated from the Yellow Emperor, was formed during the Shang Dynasty and later perfected during the Zhou Dynasty. It survived until the Qing Dynasty.

Grand fur coronet suit—Worn by the king for sacrifice to the Supreme God and gods in charge of the five directions.

Dragon coronet suit —Worn by the king for sacrifice to his father, grandfather or great-grandfather.

A tiger-shaped hat
(Shaanxi Province)

Golden pheasant coronet suit—Worn by the king for sacrifice to his ancestors.

Fur coronet suit—Worn by the king for sacrifice to great mountains and rivers.

Embroidered coronet suit—Worn by the king for sacrifice to gods in charge of households, agriculture, etc.

Black coronet suit—Worn by the king for sacrifice to minor gods.

Court suit — A suit worn by officials in the court for ceremonial occasions. In the Qing Dynasty, with the highly evolved system of protocol for official functions, the court suit became very important. For ceremonial functions, the emperor, princes, officials, and scholars all wore court suits. The court suit included a hat, robe, and decorations. According to seasons and social status, clothing differed in colors and patterns. The emperor wore bright yellow except when blue was worn for sacrifice to the harvest, and red was worn for sacrifice to sun. Princes and official ministers wore blue or azure-color robes. The decoration of the Twelve Seals did not apply to common people. Court suits for noblewomen fell into categories of coats, robes, skirts, etc., with slights differences in patterns and decorations.

Dragon robe (*longpao*)— A robe worn by the emperor with the design of dragon. In feudal society, the dragon was the ultimate symbol of power and was reserved exclusively for the emperor. In the Song and Yuan dynasties the arm of the dragon featured three or four claws, and in the Ming and Qing dynasties five, and was thus called a Five-Nailed Dragon. The emperor's dragon robe was auspicious clothing, giving way to dragon court suits and dragon coronet suits. The dragon robe was common on occasions of feasts and other official functions. When wearing the dragon, the emperor wore a matching hat and belt with a pearl under the neck. It is recorded in official annals that "the dragon robe has a color of bright yellow and azurite-color for neck and sleeves with golden leaf decoration; nine embroidered golden dragons; the Twelve Seals, and five-colored clouds. There is a descending dragon in front and in back, a flying dragon on both sides, and a descending dragon on each sleeve. On the lower part of the robe are the patterns of eight treasures emerging from water; the front splits to both sides and cotton, silk and fur are applied appropriately." In ancient China the emperor was addressed with honor as "Highness of Nine Fives", which indicated nobility. On the dragon robe in the Qing Dynasty, nine golden dragons were embroidered with eight outside and one inside. The lower part of the dragon robe was some patterns representing waves. And there were treasures emerging out of the water, indicating continuous luck, unification and forever peace.

Dragon robe worn by an official (*mangpao*)— An official suit worn in classical times, sometimes also called a python robe. Because only the emperor wore the design of the dragon, this robe features the design of a dragon-like creature but with one less claw than the

An upper garment with large sleeve (Shaanxi Province)

Chinese woman's *xiapei*

Emperor's dragon robe. Thus this dragon robe could only be worn after being awarded an honor by the emperor. Among the designs of these robes, those of crouching creatures were the most valuable. Levels of office were differentiated with the color and number of dragons, such as apricot for a crown prince, golden for princes and lords, and blue and azure for officials. In additions, there were five-clawed dragons for Rank 1 to 3, eight four-clawed dragons for Rank 4 to 6, and five four-clawed dragons for Rank 7 to 9. On occasion of ceremony or holiday, all officials were required to wear their dragon robes.

Horse hoof sleeves — Long robes worn in the Qing Dynasty usually had slits, which were also called "arrow suits," as they facilitated riding a horse as well as shooting a bow. As the cuffs of these sleeves resembled the horse's hoof, the sleeves were called "horse hoof sleeves." The cuffs could be rolled up at times or spread out when giving a salute.

Jacket — Similar to a robe and made from the same material,

Mandarin jacket

Embroidered girdle (Shanxi Province)

patterns, and styles, but with a shorter length, jackets were already popular in the Southern and Northern Dynasties. The jackets varied, with broad or narrow sleeves. However, there was no limit imposed with regard to length or the positioning of buttons. In the Ming and Qing dynasties, it was common for a woman to wear a jacket, and many have survived to today. There were single-layered, double-layered, cotton, fur jackets, brocade, and silk, with greenish blue, light blue, pinkish white and red colors. In addition, jackets featured patterns of flowers, birds, bats, peaches, and the Chinese characters for longevity.

Most jackets worn in the Qing Dynasty had round collars and buttons down the right or down the front. After the Shunzhi Period (1644-1661), the jacket sleeves became narrower than those in the Ming Dynasty, and embroideries were only found on the front and

Dragon robe worn by officials

Top: Dragon robe.
Bottom: Dragon robe

on the cuff. During the Jiaqing Period (1796-1820), as there were more types of embroidery on the hems of clothes, the jacket cuff became broader. In the Xianfeng and Tongzhi periods (1862-1874), it was fashionable among women, especially women in Beijing, to embroider on the hems of clothes. During the Guangxu (1875-1908) and Xuantong periods (1909-1911), the sleeves of jackets became short and slim, revealing shirts inside.

Robe — A long, flowing garment with a cotton lining. The term appeared in the Zhou Dynasty and remained after the Han Dynasty. The robe served as the basic stylistic element for clothes during the Ming and Qing dynasties, such as the dragon robe worn by officials in the Ming Dynasty, and the *qipao* worn by women in the Qing Dynasty. As mentioned previously, the *qipao* came into being from the 1920s to the end of the 1940s. It had many styles such as high or low collars, and short or long sleeves. As the *qipao* fully showed a woman's figure, it became a fashion statement in modern times. Among men, the robe prevailed until the first few years of the Republican era.

Woman's coat — Appearing in the Song Dynasty and commonly worn by women in the Ming Dynasty with a style harking back

Waistcoat

A jacket with round
lower hem

to the Song design. Most had buttons down the front and the long sleeve could on occasion reach knee-level. By the close of the Ming Dynasty and the beginning of the Qing Dynasty, the sleeves became broad and the collars short.

Bar waistcoat — A waistcoat featuring a pattern across the breast with many buttons. Subordinate officials in ministries often wore this kind of waistcoat. It was generally made of leather and worn inside the robe. If the wearer felt hot, he could undo the uppermost buttons.

Court coat —Worn by women, the court coat had three forms, all were decorated with azurite and golden hems. The pattern on a court coat usually consisted of dragons, treasures emerging out of water, and the Chinese characters for longevity.

Badge suit — An official suit in the Ming and Qing dynasties, featuring a round, trapezoidal, or square badge pattern on the front and back. Patterns of certain kinds of animals were embroidered on the badges, indicating the levels of office held by the wearer. Use of the badge suit was first adopted in the early years of the Ming Dy-

Top: A jacket with eight immortals design
Bottom: An appliquéd jacket

Top: A jacket with buttons down the front
Bottom: A jacket

nasty, where there existed strict regulations on colors and fabrics: crimson for Rank 1 to 4, blue for Rank 5 to 7, and green for Rank 8 to 9 or below. The fabric for winter was cloud damask not dyed and the patterns and sizes varied according to the level. The fabric used in summer was ramie fibers, gauze, and silk. In the 24th year of the Hongwu Period (1391), regulations were made to differentiate ranks and division with differences made in the badges: Kirin for high officials or imperial family members, birds for civil officials, and beasts for military officers, including cranes for Rank 1 civil officials, pheasants for Rank 2, peacocks for Rank 3, wild geese for Rank 4, white khaleej for Rank 5, bitterns for Rank 6 and 7, yellow birds for Rank 8, partridges for Rank 9, and magpies for lower levels. Imperial envoys wore designs with legendary creatures of the imperial court, lions for Rank 1 and 2 military officers, tigers and leopards for Rank 3 and 4, bears for Rank 5, young tigers for Rank 6 and 7, rhinoceros for Rank 8, and sea horses for Rank 9.

A waistcoat (Shanxi Province)

An undergarment
(Shanxi Province)

Large badges in the Ming Dynasty could be as wide as 40 centimeters. Most were light in color on black backgrounds and golden embroidered patterns. There were generally no decorations around the badges, but there was one bird embroidered on the badges of civil officials in Rank 4 to 8.

The badge suit system continued in the Qing Dynasty with variations in patterns. Members of the imperial family wore round badges while other officials wore square patterns. The badge suits had round collars, buttons down the front, and straight sleeves which were a little longer than a common suit but shorter than a long robe. The fabric was azurite. The badge suits were worn outside the dragon robes and survived until the end of Qing Dynasty.

Mandarin jacket — A short jacket worn outside the robe by men in the Qing Dynasty reaching only to the navel and sleeves only reaching the elbows, which could facilitate horse riding.

When the Manchus first came into China's midland, the mandarin jackets were only worn by soldiers of the Eight Banner Army. After the Kangxi Period, the mandarin jackets developed into many variations and were subsequently worn by more and more people. Thus the mandarin jacket became a kind of protocol suit. It was

A waistcoat

Embroidered jacket with buttons down the front

Top: A jacket edged with lace
Bottom: A cotton-padded jacket with round lower hem

common for men to wear a mandarin jacket outside the long robe. There were three styles of mandarin jackets: those without buttons on the front; those with buttons down the front; and those with buttons down the right. As the first style much facilitated activities, it was used mainly as for travel. The second style was often used as a protocol suit and the third one as an everyday suit. The colors of mandarin jackets also varied, except that yellow-colored ones could only be awarded by the emperor. From the Jiaqing Period, embroidered decorations were made to the mandarin jackets. However, by the late Qing Dynasty the embroideries on the hem were no longer in fashion. The fabric for mandarin jackets covered a broad range. In the latter Qing dynasty, the gentry and the rich often had their mandarin jackets made of very valuable and costly fabric.

Xiapei —*Xiapei* (literally, rosy cloud scarf) came into being as early as in the Qin and Han dynasties, which was a long scarf made of thin silk. It was just the so-called embroidered collar in Wei and Jin dynasties as well as in Southern and Northern Dynasties. In Sui and Tang dynasties people admire its beauty like rosy clouds and thus named it *xiapei*. In Qing Dynasty, *xiapei* was a little bit different. It was

Cloud collar

A bamboo waistcoat

broadened to resemble a waistcoat and consisted of three pieces. The front and back parts had badges according to the husband's rank and colored tassels below. *Xiapei* and phoenix hat were applied to daily clothes of queens and protocol clothes of senior officials' wives in Ming and Qing dynasties. There were regulations on the color, such as a dark blue *xiapei* going with a red broad-sleeved coat. Patterns on *xiapei* were the same as on the broad-sleeved coat, which were mostly dragons, wind, clouds, trees, flowers, stones, birds and animals. The design was subtle and complicated, the colors were blazing and the sense was gorgeous.

During the Hongwu Period (1368-1398) of Ming Dynasty, regulations were given that women with Rank 1 or 2 given by the emperor wore a *xiapei* with golden embroidered cloud and pheasant pattern, those with Rank 3 or 4 wore one with golden embroidered cloud and peacock pattern, those with Rank 5 wore one with embroidered cloud and mandarin duck pattern, those with Rank 6 or 7 wore one with embroidered cloud and magpie pattern, and those with Rank 8 or 9 wore one with embroidered branch pattern. Later, the *xiapei* also became a wedding dress for civilians.

34

Second rank civil
official's badge

Fifth rank civil
official's badge

Fifth rank civil official's badge

Manteau — An overcoat for women in the Qing Dynasty which served the same function as the men's jacket, but with strict regulations governing use of fabric and color. For women, the color was azure for special occasions and black for everyday use. The style was broad sleeved with buttons running down the front. The manteau reached the knees and colored patterns with golden threads were embroidered on it. In the late Qing Dynasty, golden round flower and wave patterns were used for decoration. The manteau has a short collar often adorned with various kinds of precious stones. A jacket was worn inside the manteau and still inside there was an inner jacket, which was usually red.

Detachable collar — Generally, protocol suits in the Qing Dynasty did not have collars, in which case a detachable collar was often applied. The fabrics consisted of light blue damask for spring and autumn and fine cloth or leather for winter. The detachable collar had a slit in the middle which was tied with buttons on the waist.

Bamboo jacket — There were bamboo coats and bamboo waistcoats. As they were made of very thin bamboo strips, they were

Knee leggings

Armor

also called "bamboo fiber jackets". The precious bamboo was wild, growing on mountains in Jiangsu, Zhejiang and Anhui. The bamboo was cut to thin strips and the strips were linked together with silk thread. They were often worn in summer. Actors often wore them as under garments to prevent perspiration from damaging their costumes. Many have survived, most of which were made in the Ming or Qing dynasties.

Leggings — Generally, men wore trousers and fastened the ends of the trouser legs. Leggings often covered only the legs and not the waist. Both men and women could wear leggings, which were tied to the waist. Other forms of leggings included knickers and ox-head trousers.

Knee leggings — In the Ming and Qing dynasties, because of foot-binding, women's anklebones were distorted and their muscles became atrophied. In order to conceal the anklebone so that the feet might be pleasing to the eye, knee leggings were applied which were

Embroidered jacket with buttons down the front

tied under the knees. On the knee leggings there were embroidered patterns of flowers, insects and birds.

Raincoat — A raincoat was split in the front and had no sleeves but two ribbons were located near the collar. The raincoat was put on over the shoulders and the ribbons were tied to secure it around the neck. The raincoat was very popular as an outdoor garment during the Ming and Qing dynasties.

Cloak — Originally developed from a raincoat. In the Ming and Qing dynasties, cloaks were made of silk and could be used to prevent coldness when going out. Toward the later Qing Dynasty, cloaks became increasingly popular and women often wore them. Most cloaks were made of bright-colored silk or damask with em-

An undergarment
(Shanxi Province)

A jacket edged with lace

broidered patterns. Some cloaks even had fur lining.

Helmet and Armor — Helmets in the Qing Dynasty, whether made of iron or leather, were coated with lacquer. There were four "beams" in the front and back and on the left and right, which were called "brow canopies." On the top there was a feature resembling a cup called the "helmet plate," in the middle of which there was a copper or iron tube for a tassel, vulture feather or otter tail. In the lower part of the helmet, there were collar, neck, and ear protectors made of azurite silk, on which there were copper and iron nails with patterns.

The armor consisted of two parts: the upper part was the armor coat itself. There were shoulder, armpit, heart, stomach and left side protectors. The arrow bag was on the right side. The lower part of the armor was the protecting skirt in two parts, tied to the waist. Between the two parts of protecting skirts, there was a knee protector with the pattern of a tiger head. Besides the shoulder pads, which were joined with ribbons, all the sections were joined with buttons. The protecting skirt was first put on, and then the armor. The helmet was put on last.

Drape collar — During the Qing Dynasty, the drape collar was worn around the neck and on the shoulders. Both ends of the collar

A lady 's skirt

A collar

were sharp. There were two styles worn for winter and summer. The winter collar adopted mink or azurite plus a pattern of sea horses as decoration. The summer collar adopted azurite with trim sewn in gold. The drape collar was worn together with the grand protocol suit.

Cloud collar — A detachable collar with the pattern of four clouds. The cloud collar was developed from the feather coat during the Sui Dynasty. The ancient noblewomen with ranks given by the emperor all wore it. However, the sun, moon and the dragon could not be used as decorations for the cloud collar. In the Yuan Dynasty, the cloud collar was appointed to the official suit worn by noblemen and noblewomen, influencing decorative patterns on the neck of porcelain flasks made in the Yuan, Ming and Qing dynasties. The cloud collars were both exquisite and subtle, and in the Yuan Dynasty the cloud collars were mainly worn by dancers and maids of honor. In the Ming Dynasty, women wore the cloud collar as a decoration for the protocol suit. In the Qing Dynasty, the cloud collar was worn by people of all social status, especially young women. There were generally eight clouds, and on each cloud there was an embroidered theatric

A pleated skirt

An undergarment

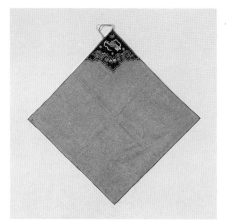

A small cloth-wrapper

story or a decorative pattern featuring flowers, insects, or plants. Various decorations might be applied to the cloud collar. The most elegant and intricately detailed cloud collar often took more than six months to make. Han women also wore the cloud collar as a decoration at their weddings.

Colored handkerchief — During the Qing Dynasty, the colored handkerchief was a long thin ribbon for decoration worn by female members of the imperial household or women with rank given by the emperor. It was in the shape of the sword and made of silk, with patterns of flowers, insects, or birds. Small fineries, such as jade, emerald, and precious stones hung on the hems on both sides.

Skirt — After the Eastern Han Dynasty (ca. AD 25-220), more and more women began to wear skirts and the styles of skirts continued to develop. The original skirt had two pieces, one in the front and one in the back. After being improved to one piece only, as there was inconvenience when the wearer sat or walked, the breadth of sleeves was increased. Thus a kind of pleated skirt came into being. Later, pleated skirts were considered more elegant. After the Sui and Tang dynasties, the breadth and pleats of the skirts increased as did the perfection of volume. The latter in particular was a striking feature after the Five Dynasties Period (907-960).

In the Ming and Qing dynasties, as the social basis for development of clothing matured, women's clothing flourished in all manner of styles. At the end of Ming Dynasty and the beginning of Qing Dynasty, there was a "phoenix-tail skirt" made of damask and embroidered with golden threads. In the Tongzhi period (1862-1874) there was a "scale pleated skirt" with silk threads running through the pleats resembling scales of fish. It is a tradition that Chinese women are fond of red skirts. As the red skirts were dyed with pomegranate extract, they were also called pomegranate skirts.

Long waistcoat—Waistcoats were usually short and reached only to the waist. The long waistcoats, however, often reached the knees. The long waistcoat was fashionable before the Song Dynasty among women, and it was even more popular in the Ming Dynasty. As there were no sleeves, long waistcoats could retain heat without impairing activities. In the Qing Dynasty, both Manchu and Han people were fond of wearing long waistcoats outside the jackets and skirts (for Han women) or outside the *qipao* (for Manchu women). Waistcoats could be worn both in ordinary times and on ceremonial occasions. The court jacket worn by women was developed from the long waistcoat.

Undergarment—A general classification of base-layer or underclothing worn by women. Often these carried more than twenty different names, though the type of undergarments were, for the most part, identical, and featured a front piece only and no back piece. In other words, the back of the body was not covered. In the Qing

A small cloth-wrapper

An undergarment
(Shaanxi Province)

An undergar-
ment
(Shaanxi
Province)

Falu daipian–a bed decoration (Suzhou, Qing Dynasty)

An undergarment

An under-
garment

An undergarment

An undergarment
(Shanxi Province)

A quilt of the Bai nationality (Yunnan)

An undergarment
(Shanxi Province)

An undergarment

Dynasty, an undergarment was in the shape of a lozenge with strips tied around the neck. Material included silk threads, gold, copper and silver. There were another two strips on the sides joined in the back. The lower corner usually covered the navel. After the Republic of China, Chinese women wore underwear to give prominence to their figures. This type of underwear was tighter with buttons down the front and was called a mini-waistcoat.

Undergarments were quite popular in the Qing Dynasty among women and children. Gauze was adopted for summer undergarments and double-decked damask as well as cotton lining for winter use. The undergarments often featured patterns of auspicious clouds, double phoenixes, flowers, tigers, etc. The background color was often red for children and young people and black for older people.

Dr. Sun Yat-Sen Uniform — Appearing in 1912, this was a characteristic Chinese style of clothing combining elements of a western suit and the uniforms worn by Japanese students. Compared to traditional garments, this style quickly became popular all across the country.

4. Shoes

The Chinese character "lü", which is the collective name for shoes, has been in use since the Han Dynasty. In the Qin Dynasty, the character for "shoes" was "ju," while "lü" was used as a verb at that time, meaning "to step, to stamp, or to wear shoes." In ancient times, there were various kinds of shoes: cloth shoes, straw shoes and leather shoes being the most common. Cloth shoes were made of silk, hemp, damask, brocade, and crepe. Straw shoes were made of cattail and kudzu. Leather shoes fell into those made of pelt and those made of tanbark.

The shoes in ancient China had rising toe caps. In the Tang Dynasty, the shoes were made of silk, brocade, straw, kudzu, etc.; the soles were thin and the uppers were shallow. Therefore, the shoes were quite easy to wear. The rising toe caps were made into the shapes of phoenix or tiger heads. The shoes with rising toe caps also had many other names.

Clogs — A type of shoe with two bars running perpendicular to the sole. Clogs were mainly made of wood and were thus also called wooden shoes. A wooden shoe consisted of the sole, the shoestrings, and the two bars beneath the sole.

During the later Han Dynasty, women wore clog shoes at their weddings, which were beautifully decorated with colored designs and ribbons. In the Jin Dynasty, there was another kind of wooden shoe: the sole, upper, and bars of which were made with a single, whole piece of wood. Uppers took the place of shoestrings. Another type of clog featured removable bars. It was said to be invented by Xie Lingyun, a poet during the Southern Dynasties Period to be used for climbing mountains. Thus, this type of wooden shoe was also called the Lord Xie shoe. The front and the rear bars could be removed accordingly to maintain balance when going uphill and downhill respectively.

Wooden-soled shoes — Usually worn on occasions of court or ceremonial proceedings. Wooden-soled shoes had double soles

Jinlian

Embroidered
shoes

Shoes of the
Qiang
nationality

which were made of wood or filled with wax to prevent moisture. Emperors in the Zhou Dynasty wore wooden-soled shoes of three colors: white, black and red, the latter being the highest in rank, followed by white, and then black. Among women, the black shoes were highest in rank, followed by blue and red. On ceremonial occasions, the emperors wore red wooden-soled shoes and the empresses wore black shoes.

Boots — Shoes reaching above the ankles, originally worn by nomads in the north and mostly made of leather. Boots appeared during the Warring States Period, where Wuling, King of the Zhao Kingdom promoted "horsemanship and archery in clothing of non-Han nationalities." It was at that time that boots were introduced to the central regions of China. In the Southern and Northern Dynasties, women often wore stockings and boots, especially in winter. After boots were introduced and used as a part of protocol suit, their style continued to evolve. At that time, there appeared the "6-in-1 boots" (made with six pieces of leather). Officials and civilians in the Tang Dynasty generally wore boots, which had many styles. In the early Song Dynasty, the system in the Tang and the Five Dynasties Period was followed. In the latter half of Song Dynasty, black leather was used and lined with felt. The boots were 9.5 inches high. For officials, the hems of the boots were decorated with colored strips according to their ranks. In the Liao, Jin and Yuan dynasties, there were multiple styles of boots with simple designs and colors matching the daily suits. Since the Ming Dynasty, civilians were prohibited from wearing boots, and a hierarchical system was developed for wearing boots. In the Qing Dynasty, when men wore daily suits, they mostly wore shoes. However, when they wore official suits, they were required to wear boots. The fabric for boots consisted mainly of black damask. At first the style featured a square toe cap and later a cusp. Boots with square toe caps were still being worn with court suits while boots with cusps were worn by common people. Although the style was the same, there were strict regulations concerning the use of fabric. The rich could wear boots made of blue plain damask in spring and autumn and wear those made of blue cloth with pile in winter, while common people could only wear boots made of blue cloth.

Banner Shoes — A type of high-soled shoe worn by Manchu

Tiger-shaped
shoes

Leather *jinlian*

Jinlian (Yi County, Anhui Province)

Banner shoes (low-heel)

Jinlian (North
China)

Banner shoes
(low-heel)

Shoes for bound feet
(North China)

Leggings

women of the Eight Banners in the Qing Dynasty. The soles of banner shoes were made of wood. As Manchu noblewomen learned to ride horses since they were young and never had their feet bound, they were used to wearing this kind of shoe. The wooden heel of the banner shoe was fixed in the middle of the sole, which were more than three cun high. The whole wooden heel was wrapped with white cloth or damask silk, or was plastered white. The fabric used for banner shoes was silk and damask embroidered with colored designs. Depending on the age of the wearer, the height of the sole was gradually lowered. Aged women or women engaged in labor often wore flat-soled shoes.

Jinlian **(Golden Lotus) Shoes** — Most scholars trace the origins of foot binding to the Southern Tang Dynasty (937-975). Em-

A small bag (Hunan Province)

62

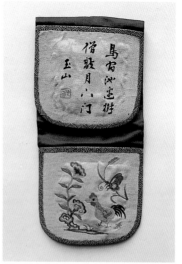

Top Left: A purse (Shanxi Province)
Top Right: A girdle (Suzhou)
Bottom: A small bag (Suzhou)

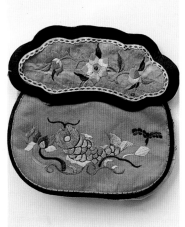

Top: A purse (Shanxi Province)
Bottom Left: A small bag (Suzhou)
Bottom Right: A small bag (Suzhou, Qing Dynasty)

64

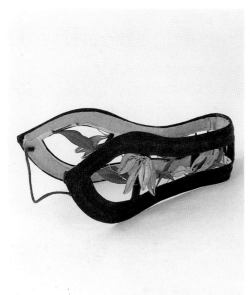

Leizi (for old women as hairpin)

Perfume satchel

Belt

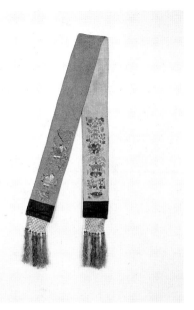

Oversleeves (Shaanxi)

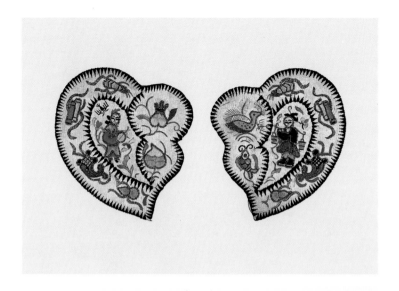

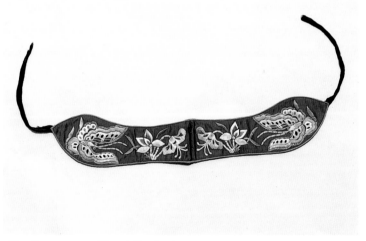

Top: Ear protector (Shanxi Province)
Bottom: Spectacle bag (Shanxi Province)

Spectacle bag (Suzhou,
Qing Dynasty)

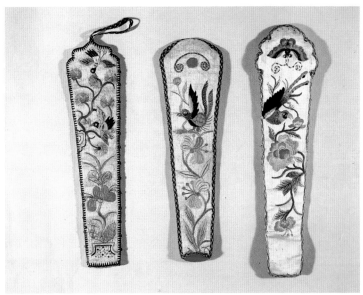

A fan cover (Beijing)

peror Li Yu (r. 961-975) was fond of beautiful women and music. He had a seven-feet high lotus-shaped platform made of gold and asked the dancers to bind their feet with silk like crescents to dance on the platform. This was supposedly the origin of *jinlian* (literally meaning "golden lotus"). As China has a large area and a diverse population, various styles of shoes made for bound feet had been formed in different regions. Generally speaking, *jinlian* was most prominent in the southern and northern regions. The southern regions were represented by Zhoushan, Ningbo, Shaoxing, and Shengzhou in Zhejiang Province and Yi County in Anhui Province. The northern areas were represented by Beijing, Tianjin and Qingdao.

Patterns on *jinlians* were the traditional Chinese folk designs, such as flowers, fish, insect, birds, Chinese characters, coins, dragons, phoenixes, the Eight Immortals, pomegranates, longevity peaches, lotuses, lotus roots, lotus seed pods, etc. Colored patterns on a pair of *jinlians* represented the wishes and expectations of the wearer while at the same time reflecting social status. Generally, young women wore *jinlians* with bright colors such as red, while older women wore black or dark colored *jinlians*.

Anklets — Strips bound to calves of women whose feet had been bound. The fabrics included cotton, silk, and damask, often were embroidered with intricate designs.

Oufu—There were two kinds of *oufus*. One was in the shape of a trouser leg, used to cover the bottom end of a trouser leg on women whose feet had been bound; the other consisted of a piece of rectangular cotton cloth or lined damask, used to bind the upper part of an ankle outside the trouser leg. The use of the two kinds of *oufus* was to cover the abnormality of the anklebones. The *oufus* were all embroidered with colored patterns.

Leggings—Women in the Qing Dynasty often wore leggings, which covered the legs down to the anklebones. There were ribbons on the leggings, which were tied to the waist so as to prevent cold.

5. Trivia of Clothing

Small bag — A decoration worn on the waist. Its original form was a tiny bag to hold small things such as handkerchiefs, coins and seals. As there were no pockets on ancient clothes, leather bags were used as early as in the Spring and Autumn and Warring States Period. In the Ming and Qing dynasties, the small bags were made of silk and embroidered with colored patterns.

And spectacle bags and fan covers were all fineries carried by people. They had in themselves rich styles and embroidered patterns as well as abundant cultural connotations. They expressed the entertainment in, expectations for and pursuit of life of the wearer.

6. Embroidery

Ge silk hand-woven tapestry — Ge silk hand-woven tapestry is a representative among the multiple Chinese traditional silk processing techniques. It originated in the Han Dynasty and prospered in the Song Dynasty. The major producing area is Suzhou and its nearby districts. Small ship-shaped shuttles with colored silk lines weave part by part according to the patterns and designs. This special technique produces cuts and holes between patterns and background as well as between the colors. Thus it is also called "silk carving." In the Southern Song Dynasty the center for such processing was in Songjiang as well as Suzhou. The works of a famous weaver in Songjiang, Zhu Kerou, represent the pinnacle of such silk processing. Zhu created a special kind of method to realize the effect of color transition. Consequently her works have been highly prized throughout history.

Yue embroidery—Also called "Guang embroidery," and including Chaozhou embroidery. It has a long history, and the Palace Museum in Beijing has the largest collection in China. Yue embroidery features a complicated but ordered design, bright colors, a shining

Hunting scene (Gu embroidery, Ming Dynasty)

Patching ceremonial suit (Gu embroidery, Ming Dynasty)

gloss, even but varied needlework, clear, crisp textures, strong use of primary colors, and subtle shifting of highlights. Some of the largest characteristic works are folding screens, and the smallest are small bags and fan covers, mostly with the folk design of phoenixes, pines and cranes, peonies, monkeys, deer, chickens, geese, peacocks, etc.

Gu embroidery — Gu embroidery refers to embroidery works with the techniques and styles of Gu Mingshi's family. Gu Mingshi lived in Shanghai during the Jiajing Period of the Ming Dynasty (1522-1566). His granddaughter-in-law, Sun Ximeng, displayed exemplary talent at painting and embroidery. Descendants of the Gu family carried on their extraordinary technique.

Su embroidery — The collective name for embroidery with Suzhou as the production center, well-known both in China and in the world. Since the Qing Dynasty, many types of embroidery such as Yue embroidery, Shu embroidery and Xiang embroidery have been influenced by Su embroidery. The patterns have a wide range of sources, such as plants, animals, landscapes, Chinese characters, calligraphy, and traditional themes. There are over forty kinds of stitches with great varieties and unique characteristics. The technique may be described as flat, lucent, ordered, even, gentle, smooth, careful and dense. Su embroideries are like paintings on silks with elegant needlework and natural color transitions.

Xiang embroidery — The collective name for embroideries with Changsha of Hunan Province as the production center; one of the Four Famous Chinese Embroideries. Xiang embroidery has developed on the basis of folk embroidery in Hunan combined with essences in Su and Guang embroideries. Therefore Xiang embroidery has its own styles of reality, plainness, beauty and vividness. It features thin split silk threads. After being split, the silk threads are steamed with soap pod liquid and wiped dry so as to prevent fluffing. The luster is better than that of hairs. Therefore Xiang embroidery is also called "fine wool embroidery". In color matching, Xiang embroidery is good at using grays and black and white with appropriate contrast, promoting the dimensional feel. In structure Xiang embroidery is good at using space and giving prominence to the theme, forming a simple but elegant nature similar to that of traditional Chinese landscape paintings. The traditional themes for Xiang embroidery are lions, tigers, squirrels, etc., among which tigers are the most common.

Shu embroidery — One of the Four Famous Chinese Embroideries. The other three are Su, Xiang and Yue. Shu embroidery has a long history, dating back to the Western Han Dynasty. It is also called "Chuan embroidery," a collective name for embroideries with Chengdu of Sichuan Province as the production center. The major materials for Shu embroidery are soft damask and colored silk. Shu embroidery features careful execution, exacting standards of detail and uniformity, and attention to intricate needlework with more than one hundred types of stitches. Shu embroidery possesses the characteristics of clean stitches, soft colors, rich varieties, and a strong emphasis on local styles. The products are mostly quilt covers, pillow covers, clothes, shoes, and painting screens.

Hair embroidery —Embroidery using human hair, also called "black embroidery." Besides black and white hair, there are yellow, brown, and grey hairs. Hair length of over three feet is considered the high grade. Hair of rare color were also valued regardless of length. Hair embroidery in China has a long history, first recorded in the Southern Song Dynasty. It has absorbed techniques of traditional Chinese landscape painting and embroidered silk, and with multiple methods, the technique of multilayered color transition is well mastered, demonstrating the feel of traditional Chinese landscape paintings with combination of black and non-black colors.

7. Collecting

Despite their often robust construction, clothing and embroidery are often difficult to maintain and pose special challenges for collectors. If too dry, they may have lost their supple quality, and may exhibit wandering fibers. At the same time, they will develop mold if kept in contact with moisture. After being mended, ironed, air-dried and folded, the article should be wrapped with non-acid paper and kept in a box. The box must then be kept dry with adequate steps taken to prevent mildew, such as silica gel or desiccant, which should be put in the box without having direct contact with the clothing. The items should be inspected periodically.

74

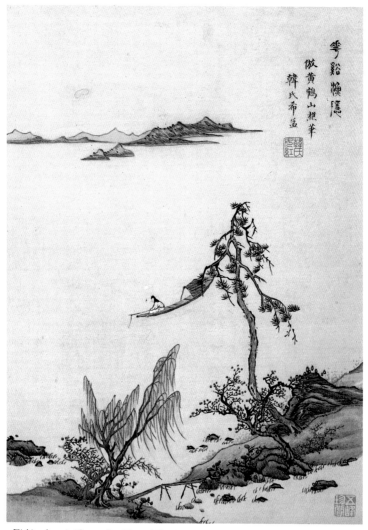

Fishing hermit (Gu embroidery, Ming Dynasty)

Mongoose playing with camellia (Ge silk hand-woven tapestry, Southern Song Dynasty)

Lake, stones, flowers and butterflies (Gu embroidery, Ming Dynasty)

An article of clothing or piece of embroidery may require partial restoration. Place the item on a flat surface. If there are loose fibers, mend and iron them carefully. Do not iron them at high temperature. Use a piece of cotton cloth to prevent direct contact between the iron and the embroidery. After that, put it in a cool, shady place to enable it to dry naturally. Do not expose the item to direct sunlight. Do not dry-clean the item. Most importantly, do not expose the article to water.In Hong Kong, Macao and Taiwan, there are professional companies that can help the customers wash, clean and mend embroidery and clothing in addition to performing museum-quality restoration.

Collectors will often display a piece of clothing or embroidery in a frame to be mounted on a wall. In this way, dust, moisture, and smoke damage can be prevented. If large items are not suitable for framing but must be hung on a wall directly, there should be several points at which the weight of the item is carried to minimize stretching of the fabric due to weight and gravity.

Chronological Table of Chinese Dynasties

Five August Emperors	c.30th-21st century B.C.
Xia Dynasty	c.21st-16th century B.C.
Shang Dynasty	c.16th-11th century B.C.
Zhou Dynasty	c.11th century-221 B.C.
Western Zhou Dynasty	c.11th century-771 B.C.
Eastern Zhou Dynasty	770-256 B.C.
Spring and Autumn Period	770-476 B.C.
Warring States Period	475-221 B.C.
Qin Dynasty	221-207 B.C.
Han Dynasty	206 B.C.-A.D. 220
Western Han Dynasty	206 B.C.-A.D. 23
Eastern Han Dynasty	A.D. 25-220
Three Kingdoms Period	220-280
Jin Dynasty	265-420
Western Jin Dynasty	265-316
Eastern Jin Dynasty	317-420
Southern and Northern Dynasties	420-589
Sui Dynasty	581-618
Tang Dynasty	618-907
Five Dynasties	907-960
Song Dynasty	960-1279
Northern Song Dynasty	960-1127
Southern Song Dynasty	1127-1279
Liao Dynasty	916-1125
Kin Dynasty	1115-1234
Yuan Dynasty	1271-1368
Ming Dynasty	1368-1644
Qing Dynasty	1644-1911